When the center light on a taxi's roof is lit, it is available.

...he American Indian is ...x Arts architecture ...once the site of Alexander Hamilton's Custom House.

New York City has more than 1,000 playgrounds.

SoHo is short for "SOuth of HOuston (Street)." Don't miss the beautiful cast-iron buildings.

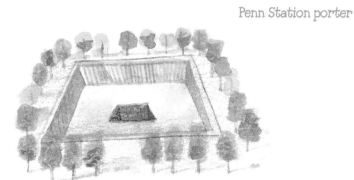

Penn Station porter

Tribeca stands for "TRIangle BElow CAnal (Street)."

Egyptian coffin of Henettawy at the Metropolitan Museum of Art

National September 11 Memorial and Museum

There are at least 170 languages spoken in New York City.

Giant lollipops at Dylan's Candy Bar

A million people visit the United Nations each year.

Ballet at Lincoln Center

...New York Yankees

Central Park has ...an 26,000

In 1626, the Lenape Native Americans sold Manhattan to the Dutch for goods wortl about $1,000.

Ovenbird in Central Park. Over 230 different species of birds can be seen throughout the year in the park.

MARC BROWN In

*For Laurie,
my NYC partner in fun!*

New York

Alfred A. Knopf

NEW YORK

One night when I was eight years old, my family boarded a train in Erie, Pennsylvania. When we woke up, we were in New York City, the most exciting city I had ever seen and probably ever will see. As a child, I dreamed of one day living there, and now I do, in an old house near the Hudson River.

At first New York City had a different name. Back in the seventeenth century, it was called New Amsterdam. Things looked and sounded very different then.

The sounds of New York City have changed. Now over eight million people live here and almost fifty million people visit each year . . . and they make a lot of noise.

The city grew to be the largest in America. And the buildings grew, too. The Empire State Building is 102 floors tall and even has its own zip code: 10118. It's so tall that it is struck by lightning about a hundred times a year!

The building has seventy-three elevators, and you can ride up to the eighty-sixth floor's observation deck; on a clear day you can see New York City, across the river to New Jersey, and as far away as Connecticut.

Once you've checked out the view from way up high, you can go down, down, down . . . to the subway! New York's subway is belowground and is the fastest way to get around. It's one of the oldest subway systems in the world; it opened in 1904. It now has 468 stations, 660 miles of track, and 6,300 subway cars; millions of people ride it each day.

New York City is surrounded by water, so go for a ride on the Circle Line, which travels on the Hudson and East Rivers and sails under some of the city's many bridges. Or take the Staten Island Ferry for a twenty-five-minute ride and see New York Harbor for free! Or take a boat to visit the Statue of Liberty and Ellis Island.

People have been having fun in Central Park for over 150 years! It's one of my favorite places. Each year, more than thirty-eight million people visit, and there's lots to do: row a boat, swim, ice-skate, play sports, ride a horse (or a bike), go fishing. That's not all: there are twenty-one playgrounds, thirty-six bridges and arches, and 24,000 trees. The park has its own zoo, too!

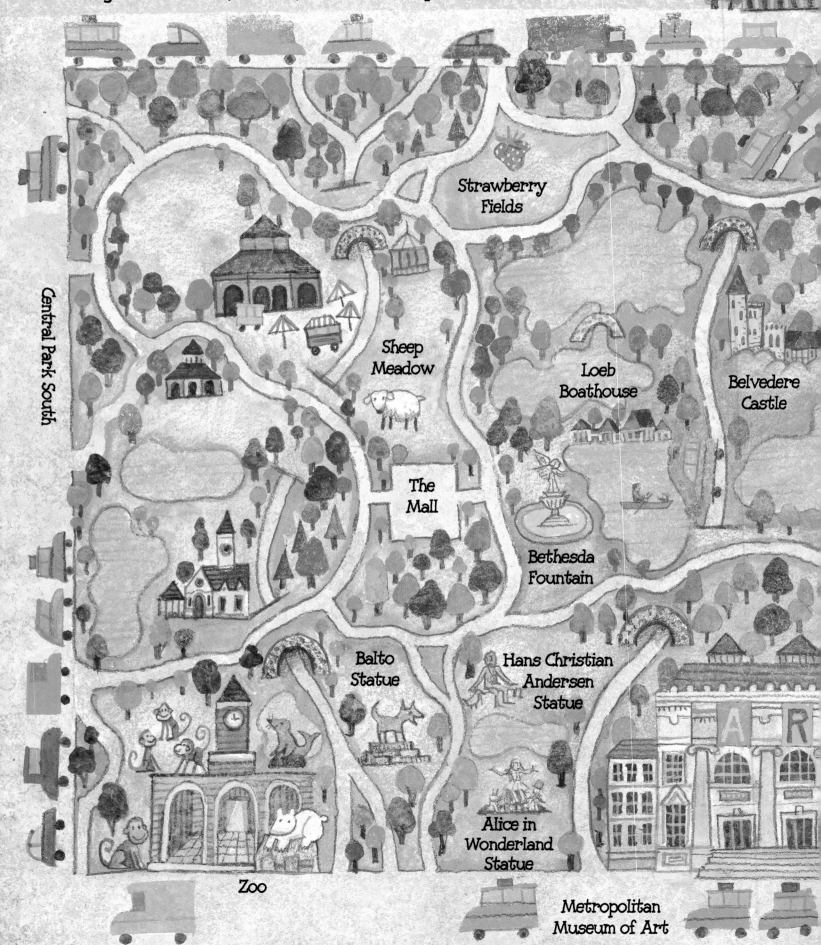

Central Park South

Strawberry Fields

Sheep Meadow

Loeb Boathouse

Belvedere Castle

The Mall

Bethesda Fountain

Balto Statue

Hans Christian Andersen Statue

Alice in Wonderland Statue

Zoo

Metropolitan Museum of Art

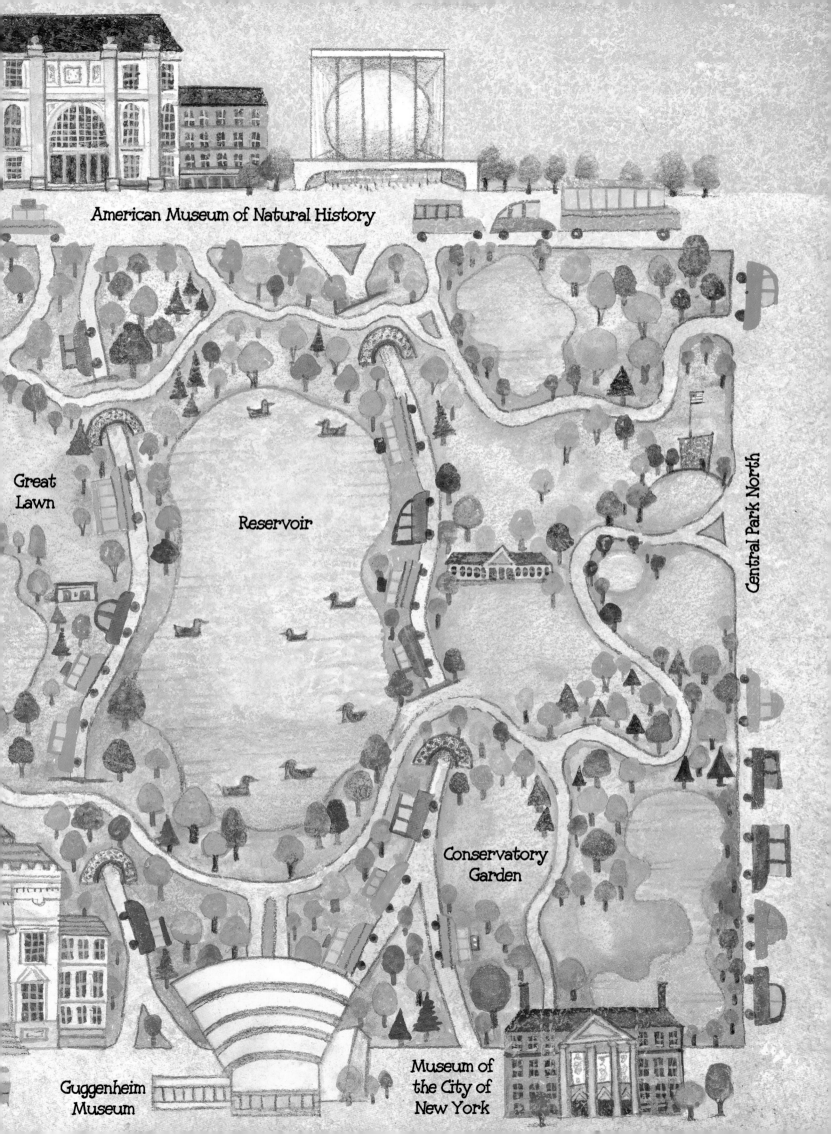

American Museum of Natural History

Great
Lawn

Reservoir

Central Park North

Conservatory
Garden

Guggenheim
Museum

Museum of
the City of
New York

Right across the street from Central Park is the American Museum of Natural History. Be sure to check out its famous dinosaurs, and don't miss the full-size blue whale—you'll feel like you're under the sea.

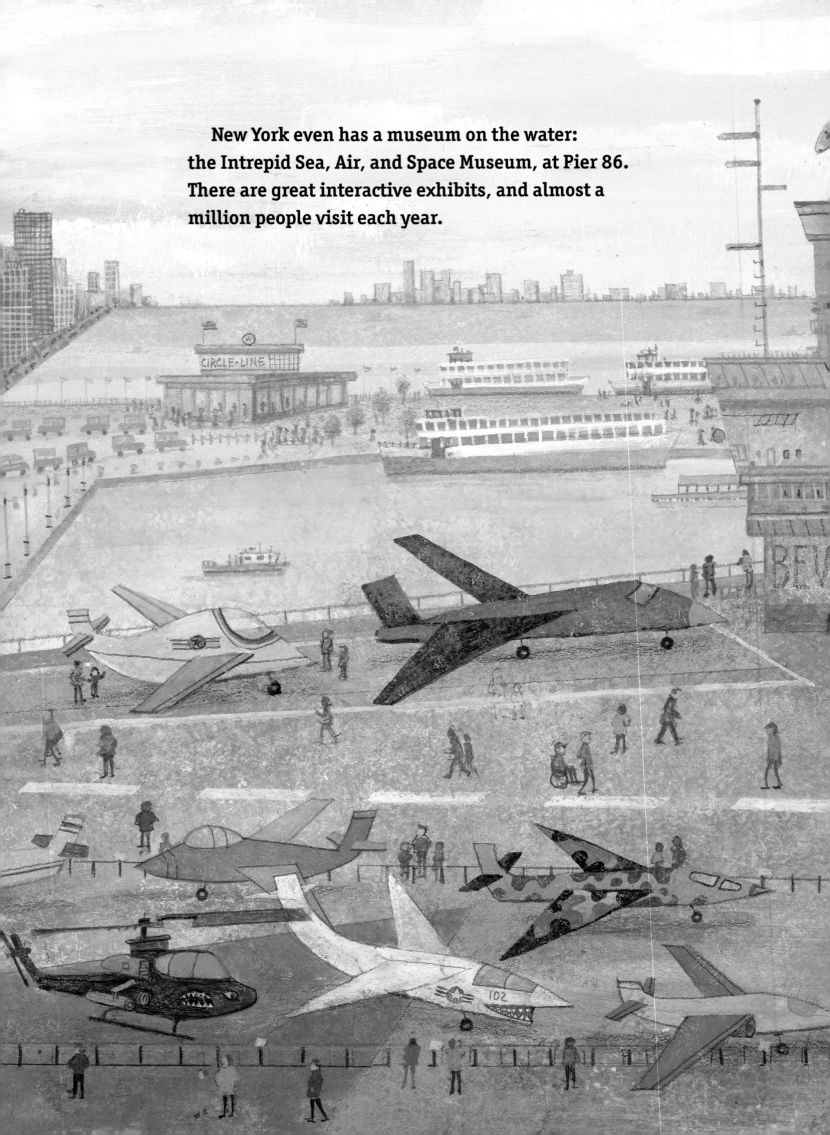

New York even has a museum on the water:
the Intrepid Sea, Air, and Space Museum, at Pier 86.
There are great interactive exhibits, and almost a
million people visit each year.

I'm hungry!

Me too!

Hungry yet? In New York you can eat your way around the world. There are 24,000 restaurants, and thousands of food trucks for eating on the go. New York is the pizza capital of the world: the first pizzeria in the United States opened here in 1905. There are over 1,600 places that serve pizza in New York.

Pizza!

CUPCAKES

cheesecake

The apple is the official state fruit of New York.

NOODLES

COOKIES

Smoothies

PRETZELS

JERK BEEF | JERK PORK

Street food

falafel

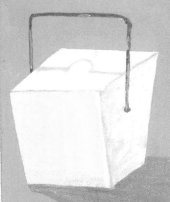

Chinese food

Approximately one hundred million Chinese food cartons are used in NYC each year.

Hot dogs

BURGERS

BAGELS

CORN
APPLES

TACOS

FARMERS' MARKET

Meatballs

YOGURT

Time for a walk on the High Line, a park built on a historic, elevated mile-long rail line with amazing views of the city and the Hudson River. I like to walk along here in the morning when it's quiet. Or try a walk across the magnificent Brooklyn Bridge. Wherever you walk in New York, you'll see a great parade of people passing by.

Speaking of parades, they happen all year long in New York, but the most famous parade began in 1924. Almost three million people line the streets to watch the annual Macy's Thanksgiving Day Parade. Go to Seventy-Seventh Street and Central Park West the day before and watch the giant balloons being inflated.

If you are lucky enough to visit during the holidays, don't miss the huge Christmas tree at Rockefeller Center, nearing a hundred feet high. Rent some ice skates and skate in the rink below the tree.

There's always something special to do at night in New York—sporting events, theater, music, dance, ice shows, magic shows, fairs, festivals, and the circus. Take your pick!

New York City loves its history, but at the same time, it's always changing. Don't wait for the city to be finished before you come visit and see it for yourself.

How to find the sites listed in this book and other places your family may want to visit.

SITES

Central Park
From West 59th Street to West 110th Street, and from Central Park West to Fifth Avenue
centralparknyc.org

Empire State Building
350 Fifth Avenue, New York, NY 10118
(212) 736-3100
esbnyc.com

High Line Park
From Gansevoort Street to West 34th Street, between Tenth and Eleventh Avenues
(212) 500-6035
thehighline.org

Statue of Liberty
(718) 354-4741
nps.gov/stli

Ellis Island
The Statue of Liberty–Ellis Island Foundation, Inc., History Center
17 Battery Place #210, New York, NY 10004
(212) 561-4588
ellisisland.org

9/11 Memorial Visitor Center
90 West Street, New York, NY 10006
(212) 225-1009
911memorial.org

New York Harbor
For information about the harbor parks:
nyharborparks.org

Intrepid Sea, Air, and Space Museum
Pier 86 at West 46th Street and Twelfth Avenue, New York, NY 10036
(877) 957-SHIP
intrepidmuseum.org

Brooklyn Bridge
For information about the Brooklyn Bridge:
nyc.gov/html/dot/html/bridges/brooklyn_bridge
.shtml

MUSEUMS

Museum of the City of New York
1220 Fifth Avenue, New York, NY 10029
(212) 534-1672
mcny.org

New York Transit Museum
Corner of Boerum Place and Schermerhorn Street, Brooklyn, NY 11201
(718) 694-1600
mta.info/mta/museum

New York Transit Museum Gallery Annex & Store at Grand Central Terminal
East 42nd Street between Vanderbilt and Lexington Avenues, New York, NY 10017
Located just off the main concourse in the Shuttle Passage, adjacent to the Station Masters' Office
(212) 878-0106
mta.info/mta/museum

Tenement Museum
103 Orchard Street, New York, NY 10002
(212) 982-8420
tenement.org

South Street Seaport Museum
12 Fulton Street, New York, NY 10038
(917) 492-3480
southstreetseaportmuseum.org

Children's Museum of Manhattan
212 West 83rd Street, New York, NY 10024
(212) 721-1223
cmom.org

Madame Tussauds New York wax museum
234 West 42nd Street, New York, NY 10036
(866) 841-3505
madametussauds.com/newyork

Whitney Museum of American Art
945 Madison Avenue, New York, NY 10021
(212) 570-3600
whitney.org
(As of 2015, the new Whitney, designed by Renzo Piano, will be located in the Meatpacking District at Gansevoort and Washington Streets.)

Metropolitan Museum of Art
1000 Fifth Avenue, New York, NY 10028
(212) 535-7710
metmuseum.org

Guggenheim Museum
1071 Fifth Avenue, New York, NY 10128
(212) 423-3500
guggenheim.org

New Museum of Contemporary Art
235 Bowery, New York, NY 10002
(212) 219-1222
newmuseum.org

American Museum of Natural History
200 Central Park West, New York, NY 10024
(212) 769-5100
amnh.org

National Museum of the American Indian
1 Bowling Green, New York, NY 10004
(212) 514-3700
nmai.si.edu/visit/newyork

Museum of Modern Art
11 West 53rd Street, New York, NY 10019
(212) 708-9400
moma.org

GETTING AROUND

NYC Subways and Buses/Metropolitan Transit Authority
511 (within NYC)
mta.info/nyct/subway

Grand Central Terminal
East 42nd Street between Vanderbilt and Lexington Avenues, New York, NY 10017
grandcentralterminal.com

Circle Line Sightseeing Cruises
Pier 83, West 42nd Street, New York, NY 10036
(212) 563-3200
circleline42.com

Staten Island Ferry
Manhattan Whitehall Terminal: 4 South Street, New York, NY 10301
(718) 727-2508
siferry.com

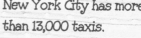

TOURISM AND SHOPPING

Up-to-the-minute information about NYC:
nycgo.com

Times Square/Theater District
Times Square Museum and Visitor Center
1560 Broadway, New York, NY 10036
(212) 452-5283
timessquarenyc.org

Discounted Broadway Tickets
Times Square Booth: Father Duffy Square on
  Broadway and 47th Street
Downtown Brooklyn Booth: 1 Metrotech Center,
  Brooklyn, NY 11201
South Street Seaport Booth: Corner of Front and John Streets,
  New York, NY 10038
tdf.org/tkts

Macy's Thanksgiving Day Parade
Begins at West 77th Street and Central Park West, continues
  down Sixth Avenue, and ends in front of Macy's Herald
  Square on West 34th Street
(212) 494-4495
macys.com/parade

Rockefeller Plaza
Between Fifth and Sixth Avenues and 48th and 50th Streets
rockefellercenter.com

Radio City Music Hall
1260 Avenue of the Americas, New York, NY 10020
(212) 247-4777
radiocity.com

Ice-Skating at Rockefeller Center
Enter from Fifth Avenue between 49th and 50th Streets,
  New York, NY 10020
(212) 332-7654
therinkatrockcenter.com

Fifth Avenue Apple Store/Fifth Avenue Shopping
Apple Store Fifth Avenue, 767 Fifth Avenue, New York, NY
  10153
(212) 336-1440
apple.com/retail/fifthavenue

FAO Schwarz
767 Fifth Avenue, New York, NY 10153
(212) 644-9400

New York City has more than 13,000 taxis.

THIS IS A BORZOI BOOK PUBLISHED BY ALFRED A. KNOPF

Copyright © 2014 by Marc Brown

Visit us on the Web! randomhouse.com/kids

Educators and librarians, for a variety of teaching tools, visit us at RHTeachersLibrarians.com

Library of Congress Cataloging-in-Publication Data
Brown, Marc Tolon.
In New York / by Marc Brown. — First edition.
    p. cm.
Summary: "Beloved children's illustrator Marc Brown takes readers on a tour of New York City with this lovingly crafted tribute that also serves as a handy travel guide." —Provided by publisher
ISBN 978-0-375-86454-4 (trade) — ISBN 978-0-375-96454-1 (lib. bdg.) — ISBN 978-0-307-97444-0 (ebook)
1. New York (N.Y.)—Juvenile literature. I. Title.
F128.33.B76 2014
974.7'1—dc23
2013020158

The text of this book is set in 15-point Sassoon Sans. The illustrations were created with layers of watercolor and gouache on illustration board using brushes and sponges.

MANUFACTURED IN CHINA
March 2014
10 9 8 7 6 5 4 3 2 1
First Edition

Dog in doggie play park, SoHo

Cat in West Village window

NEW YORK CITY SKETCHES AND NOTES

The Bronx Zoo has more than 4,000 animals.

On Wall Street, there was once a fortified wall for defense against the British.

Information booth at Grand Central Terminal

Starting in 1892, more than 12 million people arrived in America through the doors of Ellis Island.

R. H. Macy opened a store on October 28, 1858.

In December, Grand Central Terminal has a great model-train display.

The New York Jets

Building detail

The Brooklyn Bridge is one of the oldest suspension bridges in America. Construction began in 1870, and it was finished in 1883.

Gold mask from Peru at the Metropolitan Museum of Art

The Metropolitan Museum of Art has over 2 million works of art.

The Empire State Building took about a year to build!

There are more than 23,000 restaurants in New York City.

Chef, Upper East Side

More than 250 movies are filmed in New York City each year.